Following in the Footsteps of Jesus

Gerald D. Coleman, S.S.
and
David M. Pettingill

Paulist Press
New York/Mahwah, New Jersey

Cover/book design and interior illustrations by Nicholas T. Markell.

Library of Congress Cataloging-in-Publication Data

Coleman, Gerald D.
    Following in the footsteps of Jesus / Gerald D. Coleman and
David M. Pettingill.
        p.   cm. — (IlluminationBooks)
    Includes bibliographical references.
    ISBN 0-8091-3841-7 (alk. paper)
    1. Christian life—Biblical teaching. 2. Bible—Biography. I.
Pettingill, David M., 1937–   . II. Title. III. Series.
BS680.C47C65   1998
220.9′2—dc21   98-35620
                                                                         CIP

Published by Paulist Press
997 Macarthur Boulevard
Mahwah, New Jersey 07430

www.paulistpress.com

Printed and bound in the
United States of America

Contents

Dedicated

with

gratitude and respect

to the seminarians, alumni, and benefactors

of

Saint Patrick's Seminary

Menlo Park, California

on the occasion of the Centenary Celebration

1898–1998

IlluminationBooks

A Foreword

When this series was launched in 1994, I wrote that Illumination-Books were conceived to "bring to light wonderful ideas, helpful information, and sound spirituality in concise, illustrative, readable, and eminently practical works on topics of current concern."

In keeping with this premise, among the first books were offerings by well-known authors Joyce Rupp *(Little Pieces of Light...Darkness and Personal Growth)* and Basil Pennington *(Lessons from the Monastery That Touch Your Life)*. In addition, there were titles by up-and-coming authors and experts in the fields of spirituality and psychology. These books covered a wide array of topics: joy, controlling stress and anxiety, personal growth, discernment, caring for others, the mystery of the Trinity, celebrating the woman you are, and facing your own desert experiences.

The continued goal of the series is to provide great ideas, helpful steps, and needed inspiration in small volumes. Each of the books offers a new opportunity for the reader to explore possibilities and embrace practicalities that can be employed in everyday life. Thus, among the new and noteworthy themes for readers to discover are these: how to be more receptive to the love in our lives, simple ways to structure a personal day of recollection, a creative approach to enjoy reading sacred scriptures, and spiritual and psychological methods of facing discouragement.

Like the IlluminationBooks before them, forthcoming volumes are meant to be a source of support—without requiring an inordinate amount of time or prior preparation. To this end, each small work stands on its own. The hope is that the information provided not only will be nourishing in itself but also will encourage further exploration in the area.

When we view the world through spiritual eyes, we appreciate that sound knowledge is really useful only when it can set the stage for *metanoia*, the conversion of our hearts. Each of the IlluminationBooks is designed to contribute in some small but significant way to this process. So, it is with a sense of hope and warm wishes that I offer this particular title and the rest of the series to you.

–*Robert J. Wicks*
General Editor, IlluminationBooks

Introduction

*I*n The Cost of Discipleship, *Dietrich Bonhoeffer paints with broad strokes a portrait of what it means to follow Jesus.*[1] *For example, "...as [Jesus] passed on, he saw Levi, son of Alphaeus sitting at the tax office, and he said to him, 'Follow me.' And he rose and followed him" (Mk 2:14).*[2]

Levi is not asked to think about following Jesus, but simply to do it. Bonhoeffer comments, "...There is no road to faith or discipleship, no other road—only obedience to the call of Jesus."[3]

Discipleship means following in the footsteps of Jesus. Just as Levi "rose and followed him," discipleship means giving up one's previous life for a new way. One surrenders to Jesus: "The disciple is dragged out of his relative security into a life of absolute insecurity (that is, in truth, into the...safety of the fellowship of Jesus)...."[4]

When we are called to follow Jesus, life conversion is a necessity, as we are summoned to an exclusive attachment to the person of Jesus. Discipleship without Jesus is nothing other than a way of our own choosing. To follow Jesus is not a career; it's a way of life.

Following Jesus also entails a certain anxiety. Luke's Gospel tells of a man who meets Jesus "going along the road" and says to him, "I will follow you wherever you go" (Lk 9:57). This man offers to follow Jesus without waiting to be called. Jesus replies that "the Son of Man has nowhere to lay his head" (v. 58), indicating that following Jesus demands a journey into the unknown, which always implies a certain suffering.

Immediately following this scene, Jesus summons "another" and says, "Follow me" (v. 59). But this would-be disciple wants first to bury his father before he starts the journey (v. 59). This man knows what *he* wants and what he must do; this fact acts as a barrier to following Jesus. Nothing can come between Jesus and his followers. Detachment is necessary. As Cardinal Carlo Martini points out in *The Spiritual Journey of the Apostles*, "Jesus demands an immense trust in him."[5]

There is another person in the scene (vv. 61–62) who also initiates his own calling: "I will follow you, Lord...." But this one stipulates certain terms: "...Let me first say farewell to those at home." He too sets up a barrier between himself and Jesus. He'll follow Jesus only when certain conditions are fulfilled. He'll follow on his own terms. Following Jesus assumes no conditions. Following Jesus is not a contract, but a re-creation of one's whole life.

When Jesus called Simon and his brother Andrew, who were "casting a net into the sea" (Mk 1:16–18), Jesus said, "Follow me..." and "immediately they left their nets and followed him." These brothers had to leave their nets and their known life at sea in order to follow Jesus. In the next scene when Jesus calls James and his brother John, we are also told, "And immediately he called them; and they left their father Zebedee in the boat with the hired servants, and followed him" (vv. 19–20). Following Jesus calls for a radical faith, literally a willingness to go with him.

This first step is not always easy, as evidenced by the inability of the man in Matthew's Gospel to "...sell what you possess and give to the poor..." (19:21). He could not. He went away "sorrowful" (v. 22), because he was unable to wrench himself away from his past. Letting go is where following Jesus begins.

This small book offers an array of characters who evidence at times incredible detachment in order to follow God and demonstrate in their lives a willingness to listen to God. In Bernard Shaw's play *Saint Joan*, Joan hears voices from God. Responding to the Dauphin's anger that he never hears these voices, Joan answers that it is necessary to sit "in the field in the evening listening for them," and to pray in one's heart "when the angelus rings...."[6] Joan gave herself the chance and the calm to hear God's voices. The characters in this book represent an array of saints who did the same. They are remarkable icons of faith and trust.

The biblical personalities of this little book invite us into their lives as challenges to see the connections of their truth in our daily journeys, to pray to find opportunities to experience God as they did, and ultimately to follow in the footsteps of Jesus.

Abraham and Sarah responded to God's call with utter faith. Hagar too set out on her journey, listening to a God who promised to save her and her child. David also followed God's voices, hesitantly at times, but eventually with success. Ruth listened to a God who called her away from the known into a world of something totally new. Mary, the mother of Jesus, is *par excellence* the one who listened and trusted in God's word to her, and it was fulfilled (Lk 1:45). The Canaanite woman has the courage to enter into conversation with Jesus and deserves to be addressed by him, "...Woman, great is your faith!" (Mt 15:28).

Luke's Gospel gives many examples of what it means to follow Jesus. God first finds us (the lost sheep and the lost coin) and rejoices when we are found (Lk 15:4–6); God runs after both of his sons in the story of the Prodigal Son and brings them into a new way of life.[7]

Evil makes its way into these stories, making the following of Jesus at times very difficult. When faced with evil, we must "look...to Jesus [as] the pioneer and perfecter of our faith," believing that our personal struggles are not unknown to God.

The Beloved Disciple in John's Gospel is a singular example of one who was deeply loved by Jesus, experiencing a love that gave him extraordinary abilities to recognize the Lord's presence: "It is the Lord!" (Jn 21:7): the deep, human recognition sought for by every follower of Jesus.

These persons and stories are not remote from our own experiences. These "ancestors" in faith are the "cloud of witnesses" (Heb 12:1) who surround us as we follow Jesus. We need to know them, experience their energies and struggles, and ultimately share in their victory in God. These witnesses speak to us today with undiminished clarity, directness, and power. In embracing them, we taste their victory and find ourselves running our own course with perseverance.

We are all actors on the stage of life, not always able to see clearly the audience because of the glare of the stage lights. When we reach the end of our lives and our story has come to its end, the stage lights will dim, the house lights will come up, and we will then see the audience rise in applause. The spectators are the cloud of witnesses who have gone before us, now cheering us on. By entering into their stories, what might seem remote becomes near, and what might seem distant becomes incredibly familiar.[8]

Chapter One

Abraham, Sarah, and Hagar

To read the stories of Abraham, Sarah, and Hagar (Gn12–25) is to enter into a wondrously foreign world. At one moment, we seem to be looking at photographs from a family album dimmed by time. At another moment, we hear commercials for northern shrines in Palestine at a time when the kingdom of Israel had been divided and pilgrimage to Jerusalem was no longer possible. These shrines have a validity, however, because Abraham and Sarah once lived there, where prayer was deep and promises were made. At still another moment, we see Abraham and Sarah demonstrate characteristics that are all too human but nonetheless deeply valued and considered by subsequent generations.

When we first meet the pair, they are part of their clan's migration from Ur of the Chaldeans, escaping from the frequent invaders of their fertile land. What singles them out is their response to divine initiative and invitation: "Go from your country and your kindred and your father's house to the land that I will show you. And I will make of you a great nation, and I will bless you, and make your name great, so that you will be a blessing" (Gn 12:1–2).

What constitutes them as a blessing? They are profoundly marked by their willingness to be displaced and to hand themselves over to a God who invites them into an unknown journey. What further characterizes them is their embrace of the folly that is asked of them: to leave their only source of security, their family and land; to believe that they will have children when they are patently beyond their childbearing years; to trust that their descendants, unborn at present, will occupy a land now in the possession of others; to live under the influence and direction of God; and to allow themselves in their displacement to grow gradually into a loving experience of this God who is nudging them into a hazy and unclear future.

Abraham and Sarah learn that the covenant God makes with them is solely God's initiative, pursuit, and consummation (Gn 15:17). God will deliver what he has promised, and his two partners must learn to allow God to do so. It is God who announces the birth of their son, Isaac, by the three mysterious visitors (Gn 18:1–15), and Sarah can only laugh at the prospect (Gn 18:12).

God shows these two friends that he does not randomly destroy people as do the capricious gods of their homeland. God is not interested, as are the gods of their homeland, in human sacrifice; and so Isaac will be restored to his parents after Abraham was willing to sacrifice him.

Through a surrender to this God who has called them, this remarkable couple make a journey of faith and trust through a land their descendants would possess, a journey away from idols their ancestors worshiped, and traverse this journey under the care and embrace of a living God. What they knew, they left. What was unknown, surprised them. The God who challenged them ultimately freed them and formed them into models of faith and trust.

In this pilgrimage, the role of Sarah can be inadvertently underplayed as merely someone who went along with Abraham in the quest. Was she simply Abraham's wife and Isaac's mother?[1] The primary reason that Sarah is a model of faith is that "she was there," listening to the same God as Abraham, following the same impossible demands, trusting the identical promptings heard by her husband. After all, God changed not only Abram's name, but also Sarai's. Both Abraham and Sarah left the land of their ancestors to set out in mystery to a land that God would show them. They were both directed into the future, taking everything with them, including their slaves and possessions. When God promised them, "To your descendants I will give this land" (Gn 12:7), the time of waiting and learning had only just begun.

Both Abraham and Sarah had to ask, "Who is this God who makes these promises?" Their journey begins with this question, wrapped doubtlessly in human frailty and seemingly impossible odds. But even in the midst of battles and intrigues God returns to them: "Fear not, Abram, I am your shield; your reward shall be very great" (Gn 15:1).

Who are these people God chose for such an incredible adventure? They are clearly a very human and vulnerable couple. Their treatment of Hagar shows this fact all too well:

> Now Sarai, Abram's wife, bore him no children. She had an Egyptian maid whose name was Hagar; and Sarai said to Abram, "Behold now, the LORD has prevented me from bearing children; go to my maid; it may be that I shall obtain children by her." And Abram hearkened to the voice of Sarai. So, after Abram had dwelt ten years in the land of Canaan, Sarai, Abram's wife, took Hagar the Egyptian, her maid, and gave her to Abram her husband as a wife. And he went in to Hagar, and she conceived; and when she saw that she had conceived, she looked with contempt on her mistress. And Sarai said to Abram, "May the wrong done to me be on you! I gave my maid to your embrace, and when she saw that she had conceived, she looked on me with contempt. May the LORD judge between you and me!" But Abram said to Sarai, "Behold, your maid is in your power; do to her as you please." Then Sarai dealt harshly with her, and she fled from her. (Gn 16:1–6)

This story is clearly about human conflict and jealousy. Sarai is the rich mistress of the household, but barren and growing old. And quite possessive: "...Go to my maid; it may be that I shall obtain children by her" (v. 2). Hagar is younger, perhaps beautiful, fertile; and a slave. Sarai is an Israelite and Hagar is an Egyptian, perhaps bought during their time in Egypt when Sarai lived in the palace (Gn 12:10–20).

Sarai is surely a model of faith and trust. But so too is Hagar. She is a slave, she is poor, a maid, a piece of property, given away, treated inhumanely. Neither her body nor her child were her own, given over by Sarai to Abram to bear offspring for them. Even her dignity is lost in such a horrible situation. She belonged to Sarai forever.[2]

The story thrusts Sarai into a stark light not simply in the manner of her treatment of Hagar, but also in her clear refusal to let things happen in God's own time. She must take control. Hagar becomes pregnant and the promise is now coming true through Sarai! Sarai is enraged by Hagar's contempt of her and blames Abram for the whole ordeal! Do something, she demands. The code of Hammurabi would allow him to assert his place as head of the household and Sarai's rights as wife against the maid. Abram then hands over Hagar into Sarai's hands, to "her power," giving her the right to do whatever she wants.

It is little wonder that Hagar runs away and flees into the desert. Genesis 16:7–16 describes this part of the venture. God's messenger (we must remember that the tradition in Israel and in the Hebrew Bible is that there is no difference between the messengers of God and God) finds her in the wilderness and tells her to go back and "submit to her" (v. 9). But a promise is made: "I will so greatly multiply your descendants that they cannot be numbered for multitude" (v. 10). The messenger assures her that God has heard her pleas, and she will bear Ishmael (thus God names him) and he will be "a wild ass of a man...and he shall dwell over against all his kinsmen" (v. 12). Sarai will not be happy to hear this message! The whole passage is surely an annunciation event of great magnitude.

Hagar then beautifully responds, "Thou art a God of seeing....Have I really seen God and remained alive after seeing him?" (v. 13). Hagar is a superb model of faith as she is the only woman in the Hebrew Bible who sees God, and indeed sees him twice (see Gn 21:15-21). God cares about the lowly, the desperate, those victimized by human brutality and inhuman treatment. Hagar sees God and lives. In God's caring, Hagar's son is also blessed: "...I will bless him and make him fruitful and multiply him exceedingly..." (Gn 17:20).

This retelling of the story of Hagar is not complete without mentioning that Sarai again drove her away after the birth of Isaac (Gn 21:9-21), when she noticed Ishmael playing with Isaac "her son" (v. 9). Abraham again heeds Sarah's angry demands and drives Hagar and Ishmael into the wilderness where she "wandered" (v. 14) and became desolate: "Let me not look upon the death of the child....The child lifted up his voice and wept" (v. 16). God hears the boy's cry and the mother's lament and provides them with sustenance; "God was with the lad, and he grew up..." (v. 20).

The name *Ishmael* means "God hears," and certainly Hagar's part in this story of overwhelming human and divine tension demonstrates that she was heard by God. Hagar is a model of faith as she trusted that God would take care of her and her son, seemingly against incredible odds. What makes her a woman of faith is her trust in God and her refusal to give up. She was poor and oppressed but reliant on the God who gave her hope amid monumental struggles.[3]

God chooses Hagar to exemplify sublime faith and trust in the midst of adversity and oppression. But God also chooses Sarai, changes her name, and makes her an undaunting promise through Abram: "...Sarah shall be her name. I will bless her, and moreover I will give you a son by her; I will bless her, and she will be the mother of nations; kings and peoples shall come to her" (Gn 17:15–16).

In hearing this pledge, Abraham "fell on his face and laughed..." (Gn 17:17). How can such a promise become fruitful? After all, he reasons, "Shall a child be born to a man who is a hundred years old? Shall Sarah, who is ninety years old, bear a child?" (v. 17). When the three men arrive at Abraham's tent in Mamre to formally announce the good news (Gn 18:1–15) that "Sarah your wife shall have a son" (v. 10), Sarah's only response is laughter as well (v. 12). Perhaps her laughter was mixed with a terrible sadness and fear over her treatment of Hagar, as laughter can so often be mixed with tears. In fact, the text reads that because of fear, "I did not laugh..." (v. 15). It is not too long after this (Gn 22: 1–19) that God tells Abraham to take this treasured son, "your only son, Isaac, whom you love" (v. 2), and sacrifice him. But in spite of everything, Abraham and Sarah never stop having faith in God.

When the baby was born, the elderly couple called him Isaac, a name that means "Laughter," for obviously no other name would do.[4] Surely Jesus' Beatitude forcefully embraces the journey of Abraham, Sarah, and Hagar: "Blessed are you who weep now, for you shall laugh" (Lk 6:21).

The lessons apparent in the stories of these three persons take on a special character when viewed through the vision of Jesus' Last Supper narrative in John's Gospel: "I say to you, you will weep and lament...; you will be sorrowful, but your sorrow will be turned into joy. When a woman is in travail she has sorrow, because her hour has come; but when she is delivered of the child, she no longer remembers the anguish, for joy that a child is born into the world. So you have sorrow now, but I will see you again and your hearts will rejoice, and no one will take your joy from you" (Jn 16:20-22).

God never abandons his people, and ultimately our joy will be complete. The experience of Abraham, Sarah, and Hagar is vindicated in Jesus' promise always to turn sorrow into joy (laughter?) and always to be present in the midst of our human struggles and obstacles: "Do not be afraid" (Acts 18:9).

The human struggles of our father and mothers in faith—Abraham, Sarah, and Hagar—demonstrate the need to embrace one's fears and limitations, rather than to run from them. Abraham, Sarah, and Hagar had to embrace an unknown future by leaving all that was familiar. Despite their own limitations and frailties, they had to trust that God would work his promises. They had to accept their own nothingness.

Genesis is a complex book. The family histories are played out on more than one plane. As much as we read this story as a family narrative, it is also our story, a personal and even national narrative. Abraham is the father of more than one nation. His offspring, Ishmael and Isaac, become the progenitors of two peoples and more—brothers and sisters together, yet often dwelling in conflict. In faith, in trust, and, yes, even in laughter, Abraham, Sarah, and Hagar are father and mothers to us all.[5]

Chapter Two
David, Shepherd and King

*T*he final editors of 2 Samuel and 1 Kings present us with a complex picture of David. They have included without comment stories about him that are both favorable and unfavorable. There ultimately emerges the portrait of a man of faith who grew as a friend of God by being true to his own human experiences and limitations.*

From one source for the story of David we receive a particularly critical view of David for becoming king and consequently affronting God's sole kingship in Israel:

Then all the elders of Israel gathered together and came to Samuel at Ramah, and said to him, "Behold, you are old and your sons do not walk your ways; now appoint for us a king to govern us like all the nations...." And Samuel prayed to the LORD. And the LORD said to Samuel, "Hearken to the voice of the people in all that they say to you; for they have not rejected you, but they have rejected me from being king over them." (1 Sm 8:4–7)

Samuel delivered the Lord's message to the people and described the many unfortunate consequences of their decision: for example, the king will take their sons and have them run in front of his chariots (v. 11); others will plow his grounds and reap his harvest and make implements of war (v.12). In addition, the king will take their daughters to be his cooks and bakers (v. 13). And ultimately, the king "will take your menservants and maidservants, and the best of your cattle and your asses, and put them to his work. He will take the tenth of your flocks, and you shall be his slaves" (vv. 16–17).

This prediction of David as king already throws him into bad light. 1 Samuel comments, "...You will cry out because of your king...; but the LORD will not answer you in that day" (8:18).

From a second source for David's story we learn of a David who is considered little more than a predatory brigand, a man who was able to assemble a band of thugs who frightened people into choosing him as king (see 1 Sm 27). John L. McKenzie thus characterizes David as a "bloodthirsty oversexed bandit!"[1]

From a third source we read of a David who is the elect of God, the youngest of the sons of Jesse of Bethlehem, one chosen before all the other sons, the one of whom it is said, "...the Spirit of the LORD came mightily upon David..." (1 Sm 16:13).

These stories of David give us a portrait of a man of great human ambitions, profound limitations, deep sinfulness; yet still he was chosen by God. The David of these stories was capable of exploiting God's people, of robbery and extortion, of murder and adultery; but he also was a man capable of growing and changing because he listened to God in the "rush" of God's Spirit.

David as a model of faith and trust cuts an interesting figure for us to observe because his sins did not disqualify him from God's love, nor did his strategies or plots distance him from God's forgiveness. God used David in all of his stages of repair and disrepair to further the divine plan.

When the young David encounters Goliath, he speaks words that wonderfully capture his own lifelong experience of the God of Israel: "You came to me with a sword and with a spear and with a javelin; but I come to you in the name of the LORD of hosts....The LORD saves not with sword and spear; for the battle is the Lord's and he will give you into our hand" (1 Sm 17: 45, 47).

David models a way of life in which "learning" from God is the keystone to everything. When he learns of the deaths of Saul and Jonathan, for example, he chants an elegy recognizing the critical part they played in his life: "Saul and Jonathan, beloved and lovely! In life and in death they were not divided; they were swifter than eagles, they were stronger than lions....I am distressed for you, my brother Jonathan; very pleasant have you been to me; your love to me was wonderful..." (2 Sm 1:23, 26).

On the occasion of his decision to build a temple for God, David learns through the prophet Nathan that he will not build this temple, but God instead will build a dynasty for him: "...The LORD declares to you that the LORD will make you a house. When your days are fulfilled and you lie down with your fathers, I will raise up your offspring after you...and I will establish his kingdom. He shall build a house for my name, and I will establish the throne of his kingdom forever" (2 Sm 7:11–13).

When confronted again by Nathan the prophet because of his adultery with Bathsheba and the murder of her husband, Uriah, David is empowered to confess, "I have sinned against the LORD" (2 Sm 12:13).

David is confronted by the betrayal and ultimately the death of his own son Absalom, who incited civil rebellion against him (2 Sm 18:33). He is also confronted by enemies on every side of his kingdom (2 Sm 22: 47–49), as well as by his own evil of taking a census "that I may know the number of the people" (2 Sm 24:2).

When David is finally confronted with his approaching death, he gives these instructions to his son Solomon: "I am about to go the way of all the earth...Keep the charge of the LORD your God, walking in his ways and keeping his statutes, his commandments, his ordinances, and his testimonies,...that you may prosper in all that you do and wherever you turn; that the LORD may establish his word which he spoke concerning me..." (1 Kgs 2:2–4).

David's final words clearly come from a life of learning, a life often at odds with God's ways, a life that was frequently challenged and redirected by the Word of God. To "know" that one must walk in God's ways is a lesson learned only in deep humility and careful attentiveness.[2]

The stories of David offer truths about faith and life, and what we are able to glean from David's truth can surely be applied to ourselves.

The first truth about David is how he first appears as a nobody in the narrative of Israel. We first meet him in 1 Samuel 16 when we are told that God does "not see as man sees," but God "looks on the heart" (v. 7). Jesse brings before Samuel his sons: he makes "seven of his sons pass before Samuel" (v. 10). Samuel has to ask Jesse, "Are all your sons here?" (v. 14). It's almost as if the father had not remembered his last son. Jesse names him as "the youngest" and comments, "...*but*...he is keeping the sheep" (v. 11). No need to pay attention to this one.

Samuel orders the father to "fetch" this last son, almost as if he's an object. The biblical writer then tells us that David is "ruddy, and had beautiful eyes, and was handsome" (v. 12). But this commentary should not overshadow the main point that *immediately* the Lord anoints him "for this is he" (v. 12). From that day forward, we are told, the Spirit of the Lord "came mightily upon David" (v. 13). David is God's own direct and personal choice.

David's truth is of great importance in his initial move onto the stage of history: the marginal ones have a special place in God's eyes. The Beatitudes in Luke's Gospel underscore the point clearly: "Blessed are you poor,...you that hunger now,...you that weep now,...your reward is great in heaven..." (Lk 6:20-23). Mary's Magnificat likewise points to this same truth: the Lord exalts the lowly and scatters the proud and mighty (Lk 1:46-55). David is the model of the last becoming first. "Already there is the sense that God chose what is lowly and despised in the world to bring to nought the things that are (1 Cor 1:26-31)."[3]

David's first big battle (1 Sm 17) comes soon after his anointing, and this encounter reveals to us a second truth. The Philistines gather for war, and Saul and his men "drew up in line of battle against the Philistines" (v. 2). A giant Philistine, Goliath, steps out of the ranks and "shouts" at the ranks of Israel, "Why have you come out to draw up for battle?...Choose a man for yourselves, and let him come down to me...Give me a man that we might fight together" (vv. 8-10). The odds were great: the loser's side would become the slaves of the victor's army. No wonder, we are told, that when Saul and "all Israel heard these words...they were dismayed and greatly afraid" (v. 11).

David had returned to caring for the sheep and carrying provisions back and forth between his father and his brothers, who were at battle with the Philistines (vv. 12-23). When David arrived on the scene Goliath again repeated his challenge with the result that "all the men of Israel...fled from him [Goliath], and were much afraid" (v. 24). But, we are told, David "heard him" (v. 23).

David asks about this "uncircumcised Philistine" who dares to "defy the armies of the living God" (v. 26). David is then berated by one of his brothers for leaving the flock in the wilderness and for coming to see the battle! David then tells Saul not to worry (v. 32), for he will go and fight the giant, as he is accustomed to protecting the sheep against lions and bears (v. 34). David identifies Goliath with the lions and bears and assures the troops again of the presence of the "living God" (v. 36). Saul then gives David permission to fight the foe.

The next scene is glorious as Saul dresses David in the attire of war. We have already been told of Goliath's battle outfit, made only more dramatic by his overwhelming height (vv. 4–7). An embarrassed and awkward David was not used to all of these paraphernalia and simply says to Saul, "I cannot go with these" (v. 39). He then sets forth to battle the lion-bear of Goliath with "his staff in his hand, and...five smooth stones...in his shepherd's bag...; his sling was in his hand..." (v. 40).

Goliath "disdained him" for the very reasons mentioned earlier in the narrative: "...he was but a youth, ruddy and comely in appearance" (v. 42). Goliath curses David and indicates that he will soon be feeding David's flesh to the birds and beasts (v. 44). David's reply is revelation: "You come to me with a sword and with a spear and with a javelin; but I come to you in the name of the LORD of hosts..." (v. 45). The rest is history, more or less. David slings a stone which sinks into Goliath's forehead, "and he fell on his face to the ground" (v. 49). And then David kills Goliath with his own sword and cuts off his head, which he ultimately presents to King Saul with the simple statement, "I am the son of your servant Jesse the Bethlehemite" (v. 58).

The truth of David's story is our truth: the small and marginalized one overcomes the tyrant. The odds against David's victory are impossible and the terror is great. David's faith is evident: "The LORD, who delivered me from the paw of the lion and from the paw of the bear, will deliver me from the hand of the Philistine" (v. 37). Even Saul wants to outdo Goliath on his own terms—the armor, helmet, coat of mail and sword. David's "fight" is in a sense twofold: not just against Goliath but also against Saul's wishes. He must go unencumbered, trusting not in the sword, but only in God.

A final truth emerges in the critical narrative regarding Uriah and Bathsheba (2 Sm 11-12). In this story we view a new world which reveals David's interiority with all its problematic anguish, ambiguity, ambition, and ambivalence.[4]

A significant moral truth that emerges in this part of the story is capsulated in the sentence, "...The thing that David had done displeased the LORD" (2 Sm 11:27). Human conduct is answerable to God's moral guidance. No one is immune. Equally as important, however, is the statement that "...the LORD loved him..." (2 Sm 12:24): even in a family of sordid evil and a human family of sinfulness and disobedience, God makes an abiding commitment. This part of David's story is not a hopeless account in which evil easily defeats and destroys; there is always God's love.

This point is well demonstrated in the Uriah-Bathsheba story as briefly contained in 2 Samuel 11:2-5. Everything happens here and it happens quickly:

It happened, late one afternoon, when David arose from his couch and was walking upon the roof of the king's house, that he saw from the roof a woman bathing; and the woman was very beautiful. And David sent and inquired about the woman. And one said, "Is not this Bathsheba, the daughter of Eliam, the wife of Uriah the Hittite?" So David sent messengers, and took her; and she came to him, and he lay with her. (Now she was purifying herself from uncleanness.) Then she returned to her house. And the woman conceived; and she sent and told David, "I am with child."

David is clearly in charge of the whole scene, and the woman's only remark is the statement that she is pregnant. The world has changed. David is not in control. An irretrievable act has occurred. And David's cover-up begins.

First, being a man of action and decision, David knows immediately what to do (2 Sm 11:6–11): "Send me Uriah the Hittite." David gives him a furlough and tells him to go to his wife and get her pregnant (the euphemism is used, "Wash your feet"). Uriah rejects David's offer and thereby unwittingly refuses to participate in the king's innocuous resolution. David becomes a frantic man and is drawn to more desperate action.

Second, we are told that "in the evening" (v. 13) Uriah lay on his couch, but "in the morning" (v. 14) David writes his letter to Joab, and moves to have Uriah killed (murdered?) in battle. The innocent one sleeps, while the wicked man plots evil.[5] The most ironic part of this scenario is mentioned in v. 14: David sends the letter of execution by the hand of Uriah himself. David stoops very low in the cover-up.

We are told five times (vv. 15–24) that Uriah is dead and David's only response is, "Do not let this matter trouble you..." (v. 25). In other words, David announces that the killing should not be thought of as evil.

The narrative comes to an end in verses 26–27. Bathsheba properly mourns her dead husband, and then joins the entourage of David. Importantly, however, she is named by the author as "the wife of Uriah," as she is never to be mistaken for anyone else. This statement hangs as a moral judgment over David.

We are then told that "the thing that David had done displeased the LORD" (v. 27). David might have thought that the story could be played out in secret. But God appears in the narrative, and this appearance is a decisive moment. What David has named not evil (don't let the matter trouble you), God names as evil—a direct contradiction to David's verdict. The contrast is complete.[6]

The presence of God ushers in the final moment of the story: "And the LORD sent Nathan to David" (2 Sm 12:1). God takes center stage. And Nathan starkly says, "You are the man" (v. 7), a prophetic counterstatement to the woman's, "I am with child" (2 Sm 11:5). Nathan details David's transgressions: "...You despised the word of the LORD....You have smitten Uriah the Hittite with the sword, and have taken his wife..." (2 Sm 12:9–10).

The charges are unanswerable and the sentencing of David is quick:

Now therefore the sword shall never depart from your house, because you have despised me....I will raise up evil against you out of your own house; and I will take your wives before your eyes, and give them to your neighbor, and he shall lie with your wives in the sight of the sun. For you did it secretly; but I will do this thing before all Israel, and before the sun. (vv. 11–13)

The final and critical surprise then comes immediately from David's mouth and heart: "I have sinned against the Lord" (v. 13), and Nathan replies, "The LORD also has put away your sin, you shall not die" (v. 14). Nathan does predict, however, that the child born of this relationship must die.

These stories reveal the many faces of David, and each one reveals a certain truth about life. Each David has a distinct rendering and a fascinating character. There is something genuinely human about David and in this way he is an important model for us. There is a "tough faith" about him which permits him to yield to God in a deeply genuine fashion: for example, "I have sinned against the LORD." We see in David a wonderful balance between human sensitivity and vulnerability, and a profound yielding to God (see 1 Chr 29).

David is a man of stunning faith (see 2 Sm 15:24–29 and 16:12). He evidences a life of trust and hope in a living God who can intervene to make a difference. David ultimately yields his life to God, and this becomes the ground of his hope and his strength.

Chapter Three

Ruth, a Woman of Worth, and Mary, the First Disciple

Ruth

*T*here are many examples in the Bible in which God attempts to widen the horizons of people, to liberate them from their isolationist positions. God's words to Abraham, "...By you all the families of the earth shall bless themselves" *(Gn 12:3)* echo and ripple through Deutero–Isaiah, through Jonah, and through the tender and delicate story of Ruth.

This beautiful story shows that gentiles, nonmembers of the chosen people, are indeed chosen by God and can respond magnanimously to God's election. Who is not moved by the loving loyalty of the Moabite woman, Ruth, for Naomi, her mother-in-law from Bethlehem?

After Naomi is widowed, she plans to return home and tells her two daughters-in-law, Orpah and Ruth, to stay in their country. Orpah does as Naomi asks, but Ruth replies:

> Entreat me not to leave you or to return from following you; for where you go I will go, and where you lodge I will lodge; your people shall be my people, and your God my God; where you die I will die, and there I will be buried. (Ru 1: 16–17)

This extraordinary faithfulness on the part of Ruth will be richly rewarded by God by the end of her story.

After Ruth bears a son, the women of the neighborhood exclaim: "A grandson has been born to Naomi. They named him Obed; he was the father of Jesse, the father of David" (4:17). We are led to rejoice that Ruth, the outsider, the foreigner, is so deeply faithful to one of God's people that she deserves a place in the lineage of Israel's great king, David (see Mt 1:5). We see that God chooses whom he wills to participate in the mystery of salvation.

When Matthew begins the genealogy of Jesus (1:1–17), he tells us that Jesus Christ is called Emmanuel, which means "God with us" (v. 23). As we read this history of Jesus, we read of Ruth, the woman of Gentile origin who belongs to the chosen people because of her loving loyalty to Naomi and to Ruth's husband, Boaz. Not only does she deserve to become the grandmother of David, but she is recognized as an ancestor of Jesus himself.

Matthew's Gospel is filled with appeals to be more inclusive, to break boundaries, to welcome with hospitality all those who on first sight are excluded and rejected.[1] Matthew ends his Gospel on the significant note that communities of believers continue the work of Emmanuel only if they reach out to all nations:

> Go therefore and make disciples of all nations, baptizing them in the name of the Father and the Son and the Holy Spirit, teaching them to observe all that I have commanded you; and lo, I am with you always, to the close of the age. (Mt 28:19–20)

In her wonderfully delightful book *Not Counting Women and Children*,[2] Megan McKenna thus names Ruth as "one of the most known and loved women in the Hebrew scriptures though she is often misunderstood."[3] Ruth is an outsider who married in; she is fundamentally not remembered for her marriages, but rather for her friendship with Naomi, her mother-in-law. Her powerfully moving words to Naomi, "...Where you go I will go...," are spoken from the heart and spoken to a woman who has been left alone and bereft by the death of her husband.

Ruth's story is one of solidarity between people, and here especially between two women. It is a story which tells how two women worked together by using their wits and their love to survive. They become part of a people, and they become the most remarkable of friends.

Ruth's story begins in Bethlehem in a time of famine. We are told that "a certain man of Bethlehem in

Judah went to sojourn in the country of Moab, he and his wife and his two sons" (1:1). The man is Elimelech, his wife is Naomi, and his sons are Mahlon and Chilion. Soon Elimelech dies, leaving Naomi a widow. The two sons marry Moabite women, Orpah and Ruth.

After ten years both Mahlon and Chilion die, leaving another two women widowed. Naomi decides to go back to Bethlehem because she has heard that the Lord has visited his people and given them food (v. 6). She entreats both of her daughters-in-law to return to their mothers' houses and to seek with her blessing for husbands and children in the future (vv. 8–9).

Twice Naomi pleads with them to go for she has nothing, and her future is bleak (v. 13). After a time of grief and weeping, Orpah heeds Naomi's advice, kisses her goodbye, and leaves. "But Ruth clung to her" (v. 14). It is now that Ruth cries out her memorable pledge of fidelity to go with Naomi wherever she goes. Ruth's vow was so powerful that "...when Naomi saw that she was determined to go with her, she said no more" (v. 18). The chapter ends as the people of Bethlehem welcome her back. Naomi tells them, however, that she should now be called "Mara, for the Almighty has dealt very bitterly with me" (v. 20).

Ruth has cast her lot because of love and friendship. She accepts the hard fate that Naomi herself must live with—being a widow without children and living at risk in the community. In standing with Naomi, then, Ruth abandons her country and her religion. "In many respects she abandons her future for a present that will be full of hardship and poverty and being an outcast in Bethlehem—

a foreigner, one who does not belong and is not protected by the Law, except as one of the *anawim,* one of the very poor."[4] Ruth's truth reveals much about the meaning of friendship and the importance of fidelity even when one is faced with a dark future. Ruth sided with someone poorer than herself, and she spoke with passion and devotion to a friend—rare actions then and today.

As chapter 2 opens, the two women find gleaning the fields to be their only means of survival. The Law required that after the first cutting of a harvest ("they came to Bethlehem at the beginning of barley harvest" [1:22]), the fields were to be left for the poor, widows, aliens, for-eigners, and strangers. Those groups were given the "right" to glean before a second harvest or cutting. Those with nothing could then survive. Ruth goes to the field of Boaz, "a man of wealth" (2:1), an old friend of Naomi's husband.

Boaz comes to the field and notices Ruth: "Whose maiden is this?" (v. 5). The servant in charge gives Boaz an accounting of Ruth's background and how she got there (vv. 5–7). Boaz provides an understanding heart when he hears of Ruth's care for Naomi and blesses her: "The LORD recompense you for what you have done, and a full reward be given you by the LORD, the God of Israel, under whose wings you have come to take refuge!" (v. 12).

Boaz protects her from the possibility of vio-lence and surrounds her in the field with the care of his maidens. He gives her water and allows her to "pull out some from the bundles" (v. 16), and even orders the har-vesters to drop some handfuls of grain for her (v. 14), thus providing her a great abundance. Ruth thanks him with customary gentleness, "You are most gracious to me, my lord, for you have comforted me..." (v. 13). When Naomi hears of the extraordinary generosity of Boaz, she prays, "Blessed be he by the LORD, whose kindness has not forsaken the living or the dead!" (v. 20).

It is here that the story shifts as Naomi develops a strategy (chap. 3). Naomi tells Ruth that it is now her responsibility to return Ruth's love by trying to find a home for her. Naomi has Ruth put on her finest clothes, anoint herself, and go to the threshing floor that evening. She is to wait until after Boaz has gone to bed; she is to lie at his feet and then "he will tell you what to do" (v. 4). Ruth's trust in Naomi is full: "All that you say I will do" (v. 5). Her fidelity to Naomi remains constant.

Boaz is deeply moved by Ruth's amorous attention, especially since she has not "gone after young men, whether poor or rich" (v. 10). Boaz tells Ruth not to fear and promises her that he will do for her whatever she asks, for everyone knows that "you are a woman of worth" (v. 11). He speaks to her of the possibility of marriage but he must first make arrangements and deal with a certain man who has prior claim to the land. Ruth's actions encourage Boaz to obey the law and reclaim for Naomi lost land for her as an impoverished widow. Boaz promises to settle this whole matter "today" (v. 18).

As chapter 4 opens, Boaz goes to the city gate and intercepts the man with the prior claim. He also gathers together "ten men of the elders of the city" (v. 2), and asks the man, in the presence of those gathered together as witnesses, if he might buy the land. The man indicates, "I cannot redeem it for myself, lest I impair my own inheritance. Take my right of redemption yourself, for I cannot redeem it" (v. 6). Boaz then buys the land and marries Ruth, that the name of Mahlon may never be forgotten. The witnesses affirm these negotiations and bless Ruth who "...like Rachel and Leah,... together built up the house of Israel" (v. 11).

Boaz and Ruth have a child who is named Obed, and Naomi lays him in her lap, receiving the blessing of the gathered women:

> Blessed be the LORD, who has not left you this day without next of kin; and may his name be renowned in Israel! He shall be to you a restorer of life and a nourisher of your old age; for your daughter-in-law who loves you, who is more to you than seven sons, has borne him." (vv. 14–15)

Ruth's and Naomi's story is one of love, friendship, and solidarity, the narrative of a poor woman with no apparent future. Together they share this love, hope, and friendship, and Ruth, the outsider, ultimately teaches Israel what true faithfulness and love are and can be. In working and loving together, they survive and have a future. Their truth is a revelation of unselfish love and thus an image of fidelity and trust for every one of us. Ruth too is the representation of single-minded devotion to the poor.[5]

Mary

Ruth provides an invaluable mirror to the one who is the ultimate icon of faithfulness and truth—Mary the mother of Jesus. What Ruth reveals in shade, Mary brilliantly discloses in light. Both hand over their independence to God, promising their lives in service of another. Both are incredibly faithful to the Word of God. Much of what Mary sings in her Magnificat concerns the poor and the oppressed: God has "regarded the low state of his handmaiden...He has scattered the proud in the imagination of their hearts, he has put down the mighty from their thrones, and exalted those of low degree; he has filled the hungry with good things..." (Lk 1:48-53). Ruth's witness surely is a step toward the fullness of God's revelation as echoed in Mary's hymn of praise.

When Naomi and Ruth arrived in Bethlehem, the city was astir (Ru 1:19). Bethlehem again stirs when the magi bring news of the child to Herod: "'We have seen his star in the East, and have come to worship him.' When Herod the king heard this, he was troubled, and all Jerusalem with him" (Mt 1:2). Boaz had taken care of the widow, the poor woman in his midst; and Joseph the just man (Mt 1:19) acts in a similar fashion, taking Mary into his house out of love and faithfulness (Mt 1:24-25).

Ruth was a woman of valor, a woman who puts another woman, older and in need, first in her life. Even her child with Boaz was seen as a gift for Naomi (Ru 4:14-16), a grandchild who brought Naomi blessing and happiness in her old age. This truth about Ruth is so precious, revealing a kind of love, affection, and service that echoes clearly God's love for his friends.

Mary travels to visit Elizabeth (Lk 1:39-56) and thus both women make a difficult history beautiful to behold. Mary went to see Elizabeth "with haste" (v. 39) to a

hill country in Judah, and remained with her "about three months" (v. 56). Elizabeth recognizes Mary for who she is, not just poor and pregnant, but the mother of the long-awaited Messiah:"...Blessed is she who believed that there would be a fulfillment of what was spoken to her from the Lord" (v. 45).

Mary is courageous enough to stake her life on the Word of God, to have no life but the life that the Word of God wills, and Elizabeth blesses Mary as the one who believed and trusted and so brought to life the Word made flesh in her.

God relies on friendships—Naomi and Ruth; Mary and Elizabeth; Mary and Joseph—to image forth the meaning of intimacy in the kingdom of God. Mary is bound to Joseph as profoundly as Ruth to Naomi, passionate in friendship, opening up the way of God. The words of God never disappear. They are hiding among us.

In Acts 1:14 we read, "All these with one accord devoted themselves to prayer, together with the women and Mary the mother of Jesus, and with his brothers." Obedient to the word of the risen Christ, "...you shall receive power when the Holy Spirit has come upon you; and you shall be my witnesses in Jerusalem and in all Judea and Samaria and to the end of the earth" (Acts 1:8). Mary awaits the sign of Jesus' enthronement at God's right hand and the Holy Spirit overshadowing the community and making it the presence on earth of the exalted Lord.

Her response in the church through the power of the Spirit is Yes, "...let it be done to me according to your word" (Lk 1:38). Her "yes" includes her willingness to be gathered by the Spirit into a specific community, and to the Spirit's outreach to all the nations. It is little wonder that Jesus' explanation of the parable of the seed in Luke 8 refers in a perfect way to Mary: "And as for that in the good soil, they are those who, hearing the word, hold it fast in an honest and good heart, and bring forth fruit with patience" (Lk 8:15).

Within a few verses of these words, a crowd tells Jesus, "Your mother and your brothers are standing outside, desiring to see you" (v. 20). And Jesus replies, "My mother and my brothers are those who hear the word of God and do it" (v. 21). As Ruth heard the Word of God and acted on it, in a preeminent manner Mary is the true mother of Jesus because she bore him in her womb and nursed him *and* because she is the "good soil" who embraced his word with an "honest and good heart." This is precisely why a woman in the crowd proclaims, "Blessed is the womb that bore you, and the breasts that you sucked!" (Lk 11:27). But Jesus prefers to highlight her genuine greatness, "Blessed rather are those who hear the word of God and keep it!" (v. 28).

At the annunciation to Mary in Luke's Gospel, the messenger Gabriel greets her, "Hail, O favored one, the Lord is with you....Do not be afraid..." (1:28 and 30). Mary responds, "Let it be to me according to your word " (v. 38). Mary's whole life was a welcoming response to and acceptance of God's word, here at the annunciation, at the outset of Jesus' public ministry, and at Pentecost. In this fashion, she is the perfect follower of Jesus as she takes God's word to heart and allows that word to take her into the community of believers to share their lot and destiny.

Ruth, the woman of worth, foreshadowed Mary, the woman of the Word. Both trusted in unknown futures and reveal that God "was making friends and opening up possibilities from way back."[6]

Chapter Four

The Canaanite Woman, an Icon of Discipleship

*T*he tenth chapter of Mark's Gospel offers a sure glimpse into the meaning of following Jesus:

"Good Teacher, what must I do to inherit eternal life?" And Jesus said to him, "Why do you call me good? No one is good but God alone. You know the commandments: 'Do not commit adultery, Do not steal, Do not bear false witness, Do not defraud, Honor your father and mother.'" And he said to him, "Teacher, all these I have observed from my youth." And Jesus looking upon him loved him, and said to him, "You lack one thing; go, sell what you have, and give to the poor, and

you will have treasure in heaven; and come, follow
me." (Mk 10:17–21)

Clearly, Jesus loved this man, but indicated that
authentic love necessitates the following of Jesus completely ("sell what you have").[1] A key theme in Mark's Gospel is,
then, the call "to be with him" (for example, Mark 3:14);
this call to journey with Jesus is the call of discipleship.[2]

The Canaanite woman in Mark 7:24–30 is a true
icon of this completeness as she teaches us a critical lesson about the expansiveness of God's love. (See
Deuteronomy 10:17–19.) Her story is also told by
Matthew (15:21–28). We will see her story through the
eyes of both witnesses.

In Matthew's Gospel, Jesus has just been involved
in a difficult interplay with the Pharisees and scribes. Jesus
has accused them of transgressing the commandments of
God "for the sake of tradition" (15:3) and calls them "hyp-
ocrites" (v. 7) and "blind guides" (v. 14). We are told that
"the Pharisees were offended" (v. 12), and that "Jesus went
away from there and withdrew to the district of Tyre and
Sidon" (v. 21). Mark adds the detail that Jesus "entered a
house, and would not have any one know it" (7:24). Obviously Jesus was in need of some rest and distance from
controversy. But, then, Mark observes, "...he could not be
hid" (v. 24).

The Canaanite woman takes center stage and
"...cried, 'Have mercy on me, O Lord, Son of David; my
daughter is severely possessed by a demon!'" (Mt 15:22).
Jesus pays her no attention ("he did not answer her a word"

[Mt 15:23]). His disciples were not helpful in the scene. They begged Jesus, "Send her away, for she is crying after us" (v. 23).[3]

Jesus replies, "I was sent only to the lost sheep of the house of Israel" (v. 24). Matthew then relates this woman's posture and conversation with Jesus:

> But she came and knelt before him, saying, "Lord, help me." And he answered, "It is not fair to take the children's bread and throw it to the dogs." She said, "Yes, Lord, yet even the dogs eat the crumbs that fall from their masters' table." Then Jesus answered her, "O woman, great is your faith! Be it done for you as you desire." (vv. 25–28)[4]

And Matthew concludes, "And her daughter was healed instantly" (v. 28). This is really not the end of the story, however, for Matthew goes on to tell us that "...Jesus went on from there and...great crowds came to him.... Then Jesus called his disciples to him and said, 'I have compassion on the crowd'" (vv. 29–32).[5]

We have here a woman who was intent on having Jesus pay attention to her and to heed her very personal and specific request to heal her daughter: "It is a meeting across cultures, across boundaries and borders, a meeting that is pivotal to Matthew's understanding of Jesus' journey and Jesus' awareness of who he is and what his mission to the Jewish people entails."[6] This story needs to be read, then, not simply as a personal conversion, but also a parable about community transformation.[7]

Jesus has withdrawn; he wants to pray, to be by himself, to get away from controversy. He certainly does not want to be bothered by a stranger! He has left his own place and his own people because they are rejecting him. He even said to Peter, "Are you still without understanding?" (Mt 15:16). Jesus is annoyed at the Pharisees and disappointed by and frustrated with his own people. It is easy to understand why he goes off alone perhaps to look again at himself and his mission. After all, he has needs too. The woman is a foreigner, an intruder into Jesus' need for isolation and distance; but she has a daughter who also has the need to live an ordinary and peaceful life, without the demon.

We must try to hear this story from the vantage point of two people in need: Jesus and the woman. They are both hurting. And Jesus is not acting quickly to answer this woman's call for help. This delay motif seems to be part of Jesus' approach at times. When Jesus learned, for example, that his friend Lazarus was ill, he delayed two days where he was before moving on to Bethany, only to arrive and find out that Lazarus had been already been in the tomb for four days (Jn 11:6 and 17). Both Jesus and the Cananite woman are isolated at this moment, both seeking solace and understanding. The scene is brief but the time is long.

Jesus understands his mission exclusively to the lost sheep, the children, of Israel. He anguishes over them and becomes angry at the Pharisees for their poor leadership of these people. The woman sees herself as also having a mission, to save her daughter from illness and evil (the demon).

In utter humility the woman cries and falls at the feet of Jesus, calling him "Lord, Son of David" (Mt. 15:22). She acknowledges him for who he is; she honors him; and she virtually presents herself as an offering, one with no rights, but a person in great need. She asks for Jesus' "mercy": she comes to him as a beggar, "with hand and heart out on her sleeve in public."[8]

The disciples offer no hope or encouragement. Quite the contrary: "Send her away..." (Mt. 15:23), for her presence is a problem and a disturbance.

Jesus replies, "It is not fair to take the children's bread and throw it to the dogs." She then verbally places her conversation on the level of her physical posture. In calling him "Lord," she is naming him as her master, and she the servant. Like the dogs, she is willing to take what is left over from his mission. An incredible moment of faith, trust, and humility.

Jesus calls her "Woman," a term of honor and respect. She is a woman of great faith and now honored and acknowledged. In that instant, in the moment of recognition, her daughter gets well.

There is a story told, during the time of the Tzars in Russia, of a poor, miserable beggar. It seems that this beggar held out his hand to a passerby, a powerful figure with a great white beard and deep-set eyes. As the beggar shivered and waited, the man searched in his pocket for a coin. The beggar might not have known who the man was, but most Russians did. He was Count Leo Tolstoy, Russia's leading novelist.

Even though Tolstoy had the noble title of Count,

he usually wore peasant clothing, for at this later stage in his life he had adopted a rather severe lifestyle. Tolstoy finished the search through his pockets and said with regret to the beggar, "I'm sorry, my brother, I have nothing with me." Immediately the look of misery left the beggar's face, and he said, "But you call me 'brother.' That is the great gift." Somehow the Count with the humility of a beggar, and the beggar with the nobility of a Count, had made a connection.

Jesus and the woman made a connection; and Jesus moves on from there to reach out in compassion to all in need. His mission is now to the world, evidenced clearly in his final words in Matthew's Gospel, "Go therefore and make disciples of all nations..." (28:19). Both Jesus and the woman leave changed, and they have learned from each other. The Canaanite woman's truth is found in her ability to recognize the Lord and to ask for a special and terribly personal need. Jesus' truth is found in his ability to enter into dialogue with this stranger, this foreigner, and thereby to widen the self-understanding of his mission.

The story also bears a truth about prayer. The best way to begin prayer is by humbling ourselves before Jesus, and perhaps before others, in order to be heard. We must see from the vantage point of a servant in order to become a friend. And in turn, "Our image of God must keep growing, expanding, and going deeper, becoming more inclusive of others, especially those we do not esteem, acknowledge, or even notice as worthy of our engagement."[9]

The story ends when we hear that "her daughter was healed instantly" (Mt 15:28). At this moment, Jesus enters the life of the child. He embraces her from a distance, then cures the child of her demon. The truth of the child likewise challenges us to move beyond our prejudices and smallness and truly to embrace the foreigner, especially those in need of healing and care. The woman's humility brought forth a healing Jesus, one who shares the rejection and discouragement of others. This woman exemplifies well the very definition of a Christian as described by Cardinal John Henry Newman, "...one who looks for Christ, not who looks for gain, or distinction, or power, or pleasure, or comfort."[10]

Chapter Five

The Prodigal Son and Other Stories About Following Jesus

*S*aint Teresa of Avila wrote that "God does not give Himself completely to us until we give ourselves completely to Him."[1] This perspective is a wonderful centerpiece for understanding the meaning of conversion. Conversion, as affirmed by Cardinal John Henry Newman, is "a process, not the commencement of a religious course....It is a series of calls by God..., a surrender of self, an unreserved, unconditional surrender."[2] Such a surrender takes a magnanimous heart centered in a rounded perspective of God. Perhaps author Edward Farrell has captured the point well:

One evening as the priest walked along the country road he came across an old man out enjoying the twilight air. They walked and talked together until a sudden rain made them take shelter. When their conversation moved into silence, the old Irishman took his little prayerbook and began praying half aloud. The priest watched him a long time, then in a quiet whisper said, "You must be very close to God!" The old man smiled very deeply and answered, "Yes. God is very fond of me."[3]

Our awareness that "God is very fond of me" is the starting point for all conversion. This level of consciousness evades some people because of their overwhelming sense of their own sinfulness. It is well to keep in mind a story told about Cardinal Angelo Roncalli, the future Pope John XXIII. The story goes that at dinner one evening, Roncalli's priest-secretary spoke to him about a priest who was the source of much scandal in the community. The enthusiastic young secretary was questioning the Cardinal's willingness to tolerate this man's behavior.

After remaining silent for some time and gazing at the wine goblet in his hand, the Cardinal asked his young secretary, "Whose glass is this?" Taken aback by the question, the priest responded, "Why, it is yours, Your Eminence." Without another word, Roncalli threw it to the floor where it shattered into a thousand pieces. He then asked, "And whose glass is it now, Father?" The young priest was quiet for a moment and then replied, "It is still yours, Your Eminence."[4] We are all often shattered and

broken, but nonetheless always belong to God. Such a stance situates the process of conversion and the call to discipleship.

The Gospel of Luke shows a special interest in the notion of conversion, connecting it more explicitly with other themes, especially forgiveness and reconciliation, salvation, the mercy of God, and joy.[5] Especially in chapter 15, Luke reveals his special interest in conversion and forgiveness, seen poignantly in the parables of the lost sheep and the lost coin, but introduced with wonderful hope in the story of the fig tree in chapter 13.

Here Jesus tells of a man who had a fig tree planted in his vineyard (13:6–9) and comes to seek fruit from it but he "found none" (v 6). He has already been patient for three years with this unproductive tree and decides to cut it down (v 7). The vinedresser urges him to "let it alone, sir, this year also" (v. 8), to give him a chance to give it more care and nurturing. "...Well and good" (v. 9), the man replies. "Luke's God always leaves room for one more opportunity."[6]

In chapter 15, gathered with the Pharisees who were murmuring—again—that Jesus "receives sinners and eats with them" (vv. 1–2), Jesus in the midst of these very tax collectors and sinners (v. 1) tells of the man who has a hundred sheep and "has lost one of them" (v. 4) and then "leaves the ninety-nine in the wilderness" to find "the one who is lost" (vv. 3–4). And when he finds it "he lays it on his shoulders, rejoicing. And when he comes home, he calls together his friends and his neighbors, saying to them, 'Rejoice with me, for I have found my sheep which was lost'" (vv. 5–6). In contrast to Matthew, where the sheep has simply "gone astray" (18:12 and 13), the sheep here is truly "lost," and the shepherd takes the initiative to find it, placing it on his shoulders, thus not fearing to be encumbered by the dirt and messiness of the sheep. A note of joy accompanies the find. The truth here is that Jesus seeks us out even when we are lost, not averted by our sinfulness and limitations, and joyfully, not begrudgingly, brings us home.

Jesus then tells of the woman who has ten silver coins and "loses one coin" (v. 8). She lights a lamp and sweeps the house and seeks "diligently" (v. 8) until she finds it. She too calls together her friends and neighbors, saying, "Rejoice with me, for I have found the coin which I had lost" (vv. 9–10). Jesus then adds, "Just so, I tell you, there is joy before the angels of God over one sinner who repents" (v. 10).

God "operates a lost and found department,"[7] and goes to great lengths to find us when we are lost, and rejoices always in the finding. In Evelyn Waugh's memorable tale *Brideshead Revisited*, Sebastian remarks, "I should like to bury something precious in every place where I've been happy; then, when I was old and ugly and miserable, I could come back and dig it up and remember."[8] God is surely not old, ugly and miserable, but God does spend inordinate time digging up in us the precious gift he has created.

The most remarkable and perhaps most famous parable regarding conversion and discipleship in Luke's fifteenth chapter is the story of the Prodigal Son (vv. 11–32). To walk through and appreciate the fresh air of this story, we must remember Jesus' first sermon in his home town at Nazareth (Lk 4:16–21). In this homily Jesus announced his expansive vision of who was invited and belonged to the kingdom of God: the poor, the captives, the blind, and the oppressed. In quoting the text from Isaiah, Jesus focused "the eyes of all" on him as he concluded his statement and initiated his mission, "Today this scripture has been fulfilled in your hearing" (v. 21).

As this Gospel progresses, Jesus continues to unfold his mission by indicating that the Gentiles too are invited to the kingdom (4:24–27). We are told that "all in the synagogue were filled with wrath [and] rose up to put him out of the city, and led him to the brow of the hill on which their city was built, that they might throw him down headlong" (vv. 28–30).

When Jesus in his transfiguration speaks with Moses and Elijah (Lk 9:28–36), they talk of Jesus' "departure," that is, his exodus, his journey to create God's people as healed and healing, forgiven and forgiving, included and inclusive, gathered and missioned: "When the days drew near for him to be received up, he set his face to go to Jerusalem" (Lk 9:51).

We must situate and understand the story of the Prodigal Son within this journey where the Pharisees and scribes are quite disturbed about Jesus' association with the outcasts and sinners (Lk 15:1–2). God is the father in the story who welcomes back "my son (who) was lost" (Lk 15:24), demonstrating boundless compassion and forgiveness: the father "ran and embraced him and kissed him" (v. 20) and dons him with "the best robe" and "a ring on his hand, and shoes on his feet....And they began to make merry" (vv. 20-24). Whereas the sheep and the coin were only lost, the son was "dead," but nonetheless the father "ran" to meet him.

In the culture of the day, it would have been extra-ordinary and out-of-place for a wealthy man to be seen running in public. Such a gesture would be considered culturally abhorrent. No boundary stops the father's love. Conversion is complete: "My son was dead, and is alive again; he was lost, and is found" (v. 24). The father's embrace reaches also to the judgmental older son who condemns his younger brother for "devouring your living with harlots" (v. 30). The father asks the older son (the people of Israel) to see the younger son (the outcasts, sinners, and Gentiles) as he does, once dead and now alive, once lost, and now found (v. 32), and in a most loving manner consoles the older boy, "Son, you are always with me, and all that is mine is yours" (v. 31).

As Jesus reaches the moment of his death in chapter 23 of Luke, one of the criminals crucified with him says, "Jesus, remember me when you come into your kingdom" (23:42). Jesus promises, "...Today you will be with me in Paradise" (v. 43).This criminal is the outcast whom Jesus has been welcoming to conversion. Jesus embraces him with joy for "today" the criminal receives his request. It is a wonder that this man even asked Jesus for such a request! He must have sensed in Jesus the preacher at the synagogue at Nazareth who promised to "set at liberty those who are oppressed" (Lk 4:18).

As Luke's Gospel comes to its end, we read that

tax collector and wealthy from his extortion of people, called down from the sycamore tree and told that he was to host Jesus for dinner (Lk 17:1–11); and we see Peter prayed for by Jesus and weeping bitterly over his own denial of Jesus (Lk 22:62).

In Luke's Gospel a parade of graced and favored people encounter Jesus and are made his followers, knowing that they brought nothing to the relationship but the recognition of God's gifts. God has surely buried something precious in all of them and all of us.

Chapter Six

Jesus the Lord—and Evil

At the beginning of the twelfth chapter of the Letter to the Hebrews, the author writes, "...Let us...lay aside every weight, and sin which clings so closely, and let us run with perseverance the race that is set before us, looking to Jesus the pioneer and perfecter of our faith, who for the joy that was set before him endured the cross, despising the shame, and is seated at the right hand of the throne of God" (vv. 1–2).

It is crucial in our lives to keep our eyes fixed on Jesus ("looking to Jesus") because he is the perfect witness for the "cloud of witnesses" (v. 1) that surround us, the one who has engaged in our struggle and prevailed. With our focus on Jesus, then, we explore his wrestling with evil as revealed particularly in Mark's Gospel, where the struggle is presented in such stark fashion.

In what first appears as something monumentally contradictory, Jesus defeats evil by being engulfed by it. In speaking of evil, the Gospel is not talking about something that is "nasty" or "not nice" or even "bad," but something, some force or presence, so strong and irrational that the human person is genuinely threatened by its existence. We cannot predict its appearances nor control them once they appear.

Evil lurks below the calm surface of the water and suddenly shows itself: "And a great storm of wind arose, and the waves beat into the boat, so that the boat was already filling" (Mk 4:37). Evil is that which dehumanizes people and even makes them monstrous:

> And when he came out of the boat, there met him out of the tombs a man with an unclean spirit, who lived among the tombs; and no one could bind him any more, even with a chain; for he had often been bound with fetters and chains, but the chains he wrenched apart, and the fetters he broke in pieces; and no one had the strength to subdue him. Night and day among the tombs and on the mountains he was always crying out, and bruising himself with stones. (Mk 5:2–5)

It is evil that tortured the man at Capernaum (Mk 1:21–25), that prevented Simon's mother-in-law from serving the Sabbath meal (Mk 1:29–31), that kept the leper from contact with loved ones and society (Mk 1:40–45), that paralyzed a man much loved by his friends (Mk 2:1–12), that afflicted the woman with the hemorrhage (Mk 5:25–34), that plunged Jairus and his household into grief over his daughter's death (Mk 5:38).

Present to confront this withering assault of evil, Jesus is acknowledged by God as his Son, "You are my beloved Son; with you I am well pleased" (1:11) and likewise acknowledged by the forces of evil as "Jesus, Son of the Most High God" (5:7).

Jesus' ministry in Mark's Gospel is a constant battle with the forces of evil. Driven by the Spirit into the desert, the abode of evil, "...he was in the wilderness forty days, tempted by Satan; and he was with the wild beasts, and the angels ministered to him" (1:13). Here Jesus confronts the irrational, strong and disruptive forces of evil, and defeats them. His life and ministry will prevail over all evil forces that cause human dread for "...no one can enter a strong man's house and plunder his goods, unless he first binds the strong man..." (3:27).

In Jesus the kingdom of God has already broken into the lives of all human beings: "The time is fulfilled, and the kingdom of God is at hand..." (1:15). Jesus is the "strong man" who quiets all evil and fears of evil: "Be silent, and come out of him" (1:25); "Be clean" (1:41); "...Your sins are forgiven....Take up your pallet and walk" (2:5 and 11); "'Stretch out your hand'...and his hand was restored" (3:5); "'Peace! Be still'....And the wind ceased, and there was great calm" (4:39); "Come out of the man, you unclean spirit!"

(5:8); "Daughter, your faith has made you well; go in peace, and be healed of your disease" (5:34); "Little girl, I say to you, arise" (5:41); "'Be opened.' And his ears were opened, his tongue was released, and he spoke plainly" (7:34–35); and "You dumb and deaf spirit, I command you, come out of him, and never enter him again" (9:25).

Jesus' power over evil and unclean spirits prepared his followers for the ultimate fate of Jesus. Three times in Mark's teaching on discipleship (8:22–10:52), Jesus predicts his condemnation, passion, and death: for example, "...the Son of Man will be delivered to the chief priests and the scribes, and they will condemn him to death, and deliver him to the Gentiles; and they will mock him, and spit upon him, and scourge him, and kill him; and after three days he will rise" (10:33–34).

His followers had enormous difficulty accepting this prediction. Peter "took him, and began to rebuke him" (8:32) and others began to discuss who was the greatest among them (9:34), while James and John asked to be seated "one at your right hand and one at your left, in your glory" (10:37). They did not grasp Jesus' power over evil alongside his willingness to allow evil to engulf him.

Jesus lived out this conflict with little explanation. He prayed in Gethsemane, "Abba, Father, all things are possible to thee; remove this cup from me; yet not what I will, but what thou wilt" (14:36). Fortified by this prayer, Jesus is empowered to say, "Rise, let us be going; see, my betrayer is at hand" (14:42).

When crucified, Jesus is mocked by those passing by, as well as by the chief priests and scribes. Even "those who were crucified with him...reviled him" (15:32). Dying alone, with only naked faith in Abba, Father, overwhelmed by the evil he opposed all his life, he simply uttered the words of Psalm 22, "My God, my God, why hast thou forsaken me?" (15:35). In this cry, however, Jesus sensed the whole message of this Psalm: "But thou, O LORD, be not far off! O thou my help, hasten to my aid" (v. 19). It is this "facing" Jesus on the cross that prompted the centurion's incredible profession of faith, "Truly this man was the Son of God!" (15:39).

What truth do we learn from all of this? To defeat evil as it wells up in our own lives we must trust the God and Father of Jesus. God alone is able to draw light out of darkness, healing out of sickness, forgiveness out of guilt, and community out of alienation.

At the beginning of Mark's section on discipleship, Jesus cures a blind man in stages: "Do you see anything?" (8:23). Looking up the man replies, "'I see men; but they look like trees, walking.' Then again he laid his hands upon his eyes; and he looked intently and was restored, and saw everything clearly" (vv. 24–25). Jesus is committed to opening our eyes over the course of a lifetime as we enter into discipleship with him. Only he can make us see and think the way God does (see 8:33).

Our own struggles with evil are not unknown to the Lord. He himself said, "You will all fall away; for it is written, 'I will strike the shepherd, and the sheep will be scattered.' But after I am raised up, I will go before you to Galilee" (Mk 14:27; see Mk 16:6–7). The risen Lord will reconcile and gather together his failed and flawed followers. If we keep our eyes fixed on Jesus, the architect and perfecter of faith, he will empower us to defeat evil in the same way he himself did.

In his homily in Baltimore in October 1995, Pope John Paul II said, "There is no evil to be faced that Christ does not face with us. There is no enemy that Christ has not already conquered. There is no cross to bear that Christ has not already borne for us, and does not now bear with us." This point exemplifies clearly the message about evil in Mark's Gospel.

There is an inscription that was found on the walls of a cellar in Cologne, Germany, where some Jewish people hid from the Nazis: "I believe in the sun even when it is not shining. I believe in love when feeling it not. I believe in God even when He is silent." This profound statement of faith mirrors the great Jewish prayer *Ani Mamin*: "I believe with perfect faith in the coming of the Messiah. And even though he tarry, still will I believe."

When the forces of evil seem to be just too much, we need to recall that Jesus has conquered evil and vindicated us in God's sight. Cardinal Joseph Bernardin's final testament provides a fitting closure to this truth:

> It is quite clear that I will not be alive in the spring. But I will soon experience new life in a different way. Although I do not know what to expect in the afterlife, I do know that just as God has called me to serve him to the best of my ability throughout my life on earth, he is now calling me home.

I BELIEVE IN THE SUN
EVEN WHEN IT IS NOT
SHINING

I BELIEVE IN LOVE WHEN
FEELING IT NOT

I BELIEVE IN GOD
EVEN WHEN HE
IS SILENT

Many people have asked me to tell them about heaven and the afterlife. I sometimes smile at the request because I do not know any more than they do. Yet, when one young man asked if I looked forward to being united with God and all those who have gone before me, I made a connection to something....The first time I traveled with my mother and sister to my parents' homeland of Tonadico di Primiero, in northern Italy, I felt as if I had been there before. After years of looking through my mother's photo albums, I knew the mountains, the land, the houses, the people. As soon as we entered the valley, I said, "My God, I know this place. I am home." Somehow I think crossing from this life into life eternal will be similar. I will be home.[1]

Chapter Seven

The Beloved Disciple

*I*n her book on the spirituality of contemporary religious life, Joan Chittister, O.S.B., relates a story described in The Sayings of the Desert Monastics:

> Once upon a time, Abba Lot went to see Abba Joseph and said, "Abba, as much as I am able I practice a small rule, all the little fasts, some prayer and meditation, and remain quiet, and as much as possible I keep my thoughts clean. What else should I do?" Then the old monastic stood up and stretched out his hands toward heaven, and his fingers became like ten torches of flame. And he said, "Why not be completely turned into fire?"[1]

Perhaps there is no single disciple in the New Testament who better exemplifies this level of completeness and totality than the Beloved Disciple. He is mentioned at critical points within the Gospel of John:

• In John 13:23:..."One of his disciples, whom Jesus loved, was lying close to the breast of Jesus..." (see also v. 25).

• In John 18:15–16:..."Simon Peter followed Jesus, and so did another disciple. As this disciple was known to the high priest,[2] he entered the court of the high priest along with Jesus, while Peter stood outside at the door. So the other disciple...went out and spoke to the maid who kept the door, and brought Peter in."

• In John 19:26–27: "When Jesus saw his mother, and the disciple whom he loved standing near, he said to his mother, 'Woman, behold your son!' Then he said to the disciple, 'Behold, your mother!' And from that hour the disciple took her to his own home."

• In John 20:1–8: "Now on the first day of the week Mary Magdalene came to the tomb early...and saw that the stone had been taken away from the tomb. So she ran, and went to Simon Peter and the other disciple, the one whom Jesus loved....Peter then came out with the other disciple, and they went toward the tomb. They both ran, but the other disciple outran Peter and reached the tomb first; and stooping to look in he saw the linen cloths lying there, but he did not go in. Then Simon Peter came...and went into the tomb; he saw the linen cloths lying, and the napkin, which had been on his head, not lying with the linen cloths but rolled up in a place by itself.

Then the other disciple, who reached the tomb first, also went in, and he saw and believed...."[3]

• In John 21:7:..."That disciple whom Jesus loved said to Peter, 'It is the Lord!'"

• In John 21:20–23:..."Peter turned and saw following them the disciple whom Jesus loved, who had lain close to his breast at the supper....When Peter saw him, he said to Jesus, 'Lord what about this man?' Jesus said to him, 'If it is my will that he remain until I come, what is that to you? Follow me!' The saying spread abroad among the brethren that this disciple was not to die...."

Clearly this unnamed Beloved Disciple (absent from the Synoptics) assumes great importance in John's Gospel, not solely as an individual, but also as a symbol for the community who first heard the Gospel tradition and passed it on. In fact, because of the enigmatic saying of Jesus about John in verses 20–23 of chapter 21, Raymond E. Brown, S.S., points out that "with his death the faith of some [Johannine Christians] was shaken."[4]

This disciple sustains an exceptional relationship with Jesus. At the Last Supper, he leans against Jesus' breast to speak to him. This is a relationship comparable to that of the Word with God: "No one has ever seen God; the only Son, who is in the bosom of the Father, he has made him known" (Jn 1:18). This disciple enjoys all the intimacy, disclosure, and tenderness revealed in the prologue to John's Gospel, which is the signature of the relationship enjoyed by the Word with God (see Jn 1:1–2). These words of the Fourth Gospel apply in a preeminent way to the Beloved Disciple: "No longer do I call you servants, for the servant does not know what his master is doing; but I have called you friends, for all that I have heard from my Father I have made known to you" (15:15).

As deeply loved by the Lord, this disciple is enabled to discern the empowering word of the risen Lord when the net becomes full of fish and he cries out, "It is the Lord!" (21:7). The truth revealed in the life of this disciple is that the love of Jesus empowers one to discern the Lord's presence and to bear witness to the risen Jesus ("He who saw...has borne witness—his testimony is true, and he knows that he tells the truth...") [19:35]. Two particular examples in the Fourth Gospel help us to see this power of discernment.

First, as Jesus hangs on the cross, two persons experience the revelatory word that creates the church community. Jesus addresses his mother as "Woman" (19:26), reminding us of the other time when Jesus addressed her in this fashion, at the wedding feast in Cana of Galilee (Jn 2:4), when Jesus' hour had not yet come (v. 4; see Jn 16:32). At that time, she responded with wisdom, "Do whatever he tells you" (2:5). This discernment serves her well at the foot of the cross when she allows the Beloved Disciple to embrace her. Thus she becomes a member and mother of the Church community.

The disciple hears and responds to a similar phrase, "Behold, your mother!" (19:27). We are told that "from that hour" the disciple takes her into his home[5] (v. 27). In embracing Mary in this fashion, the disciple is taking her "into his own," that is, into discipleship in the community of the Church. It is within this community

that the risen Lord continues his salvific presence. The disciple thus brings Mary, as mother and woman, into the Church community as disciple.

Second, the disciple bears a privileged position at the Last Supper. He is loved by Jesus and reclines close to his breast (13:23). Peter surely has a first and honored place in the Church community, as he is told by Jesus to "Feed my lambs" and "Tend my sheep" (21:15–17) and to know that his death will mirror Jesus' and in this way he will "glorify God" (21:19).

But the final word in this Gospel, however, is about the Beloved Disciple. Raymond Brown remarks, "The last word of Jesus...is not about Peter but about the Beloved Disciple. He is given no role of authority, but he retains a primacy in being loved, which is more important in this Gospel. To this disciple is held open the possibility of being there when Jesus returns. Symbolically that would be the final fruit of the Resurrection: a believing community of Christian disciples that would remain until the last days."[6]

The Beloved Disciple represents this community completely and is a constant reminder to us that in the Gospel of John everything must be subordinated to the love of Jesus.

In Nikos Kazantzakis's novel about the life of Saint Francis of Assisi, he relates the parable of the man who died and went to heaven and was asked before entering, "Who's there?" He replied, "I am, Lord." He was told to return to earth and relive his life. After completing this second journey, he again went to heaven and was asked, "Who's there?" He repeated, "I am, Lord." The man was sent away for the second time. During this final journey through life, he thought carefully and wisely about his life, and when he died this time and went to heaven, the question was the same, "Who's there?" but the answer was very different: "You are, Lord." He was then welcomed into the Kingdom.[7]

The Beloved Disciple, the one Jesus loved, teaches us the truth revealed in this parable, that life is a matter of centering ourselves on the love of Jesus, which in turns empowers us to discern his presence, to build up the community of the Church, and to become followers.

Conclusion

As we conclude these stories and journeys of conversion and discipleship presented by the Bible, we hope that the Word of God itself has shed light on our own human experiences. Ambiguous, murky, threatened by withering evil, confused and confusing as these experiences might be, they can also be the opportunity for conversion and authentic growth and intimacy with God.

- Like Abraham, Sarah, and Hagar, we may be displaced, exiled and threatened;
- Like David, we may be a complex mixture of the noble and the profane;

• Like Ruth, we may be asked to stretch our embrace to be more inclusive and hospitable;

• Like Mary, we may be asked to trust that the Word of God will give us the experience of the risen Jesus;

• Like the characters in the parables of Jesus, we may be overwhelmed by the mercy of God and left trembling with tenderness;

• Like Jesus himself, we may find ourselves opposing the onslaught of evil that seems at times impossible to resist;

• Like the Beloved Disciple, we may be called to experience profound intimacy with Jesus.

Whatever our human situation, the Word of God promises that God is present to us in all the exigencies of our lives. As in the crucifixion itself, the personal crosses we experience as followers of Jesus can be precisely the places where God is most at work renewing and redirecting our human efforts and hopes.

Notes

Introduction

    1. Dietrich Bonhoeffer, *The Cost of Discipleship* (London: SCM Press Ltd., 1959), esp. pp. 48–68.

    2. We cite the Revised Standard Version of the Bible throughout the book.

    3. Bonhoeffer, *Cost of Discipleship*, p. 49.

    4. Ibid.

    5. Carlo M. Martini, S.J., *The Spiritual Journey of the Apostles* (Boston: St. Paul Books and Media, 1991), p. 39.

    6. Bernard Shaw, *Saint Joan* (New York: The Modern Library), p. 118.

    7. See William J. O'Malley, "The Moral Practice of Jesus," *America* 170 (1994): 8–11, esp. 10–11.

    8. T. S. Eliot captures this point in "Tradition and the Individual Talent": "Someone once said, 'The dead writers are remote from us because we *know* so much more than they did.' Precisely, and they are that which we

know." T. S. Eliot, *Selected Essays* (New York: Harcourt, Brace and World, Inc.), 1960, p. 6.

Chapter One. Abraham, Sarah, and Hagar

1. We have gleaned insights about Sarah from Megan McKenna's wonderful book, *Not Counting Women and Children: Neglected Stories from the Bible* (New York: Orbis Books, 1994), pp. 169–89.

2. McKenna points out that only Hebrew slaves might be set free in the seventh or jubilee years; foreigners stayed slaves. The law gave no hope to pagans. Hagar was lost.

3. McKenna insightfully remarks, "Faith is an undying hope in freedom, obedience to the vision and the word of God, and fierce tenderness toward the weak, the poor, the slaves whose faces reveal Yahweh, Jesus, and the Spirit. Faith is hearing the cries of the poor, siding with them, giving them vision and a future. Faith is knowing that no one can be allowed to remain abused and treated inhumanely by anyone else. Faith is relying on God when there is no one else there, not even those who claim to be people of faith" (p. 188).

4. See Frederick Buechner's delightful treatment of Abraham and Sarah in *Peculiar Treasures* (San Francisco: Harper, 1979).

5. See Burton L. Visotzky, *The Genesis of Ethics* (New York: Crown Publishers, Inc., 1996), especially chap. 2–5.

Chapter Two. David, Shepherd and King

1. John L. McKenzie, *The Old Testament Without Illusion* (Chicago: Thomas More Press, 1979), p. 236.

2. See Walter Brueggemann, *David's Truth in Israel's Imagination and Memory* (New York: Fortress Press, 1985), p. 13. Brueggemann wisely remarks that "Israel is fascinated by David, deeply attracted to him, bewildered by him, occasionally embarrassed by him, but never disowning him....His memory and presence keep generating more and more stories....He is a person who fits David Tracy's notion of a 'classic,' surrounded by a community that continually returns to him for authority, not doubting that there is more yet to be given" (p. 13).

3. Ibid., p. 28.

4. Ibid., pp. 43–65. From this time on we see in the story the clear manifestations of the prediction in 2 Samuel 12:10: "Now therefore the sword shall never depart from your house, because you have despised me...."

5. See Micah 2:1, "Woe to those who devise wickedness and work evil upon their beds! When the morning dawns, they perform it, because it is in the power of their hand."

6. Here David practices the very thing the prophets condemn: "Woe to those who call evil good and good evil, who put darkness for light..." (Is 5:20), and "Seek good, and not evil, that you may live; and so the LORD, the God of hosts, will be with you..." (Am 5:14).

Chapter Three. Ruth, a Woman of Worth, and
Mary, the First Disciple

1. See, e.g., the story of the Canaanite women (15:21–32), and the parable about the lost sheep (18:10–14).

2. Megan McKenna, *Not Counting Women and Children* (New York: Orbis Books, 1994), pp. 105–12.

3. Ibid., p. 105. We record here the insights of McKenna.

4. Ibid., p. 106.

5. McKenna remarks, "Ruth's generosity, her honorableness even in poverty, her dignity and her choice, her options in another's even more desparate need, and her love win her a place in Jesus' family tree. Her charity and her mercy make her memorable. [She]...teaches faithfulness, tender-hearted love, and hard-headed attention to life. Some say that she is one of the first to make the option for the poor." *Not Counting Women.*, 109–10.

6. Ibid., p. 112.

Chapter Four. The Canaanite Woman, an
Icon of Discipleship

1. This theme constitutes the basic explanation of chapter 1 of *Veritatis Splendor*, John Paul II, *Origins* 23 (1993): 300–307.

2. See Carlo M. Martini, S.J., *The Spiritual Journey of the Apostles* (Boston: St. Paul Books and Media, 1991), esp. pp. 11–14.

3. See "The Canaanite Woman" in Megan McKenna's *Not Counting Women and Children* (New York:

Orbis Books, 1994), pp. 121–43. We will follow closely McKenna's challenging interpretation of these texts.

4. Compare this text with Mark's account in 7:26–30.

5. The same point is made in Mark 7:31–37 and 8:1–2.

6. McKenna, *Not Counting Women*, p. 121.

7. For a very helpful interpretation of this scene, see John Shea, *Gospel Light* (New York: Crossroad Publishing Co., 1998), pp. 68–76.

8. Ibid., pp. 128–29.

9. Ibid., p. 134.

10. Cited in Vincent Ferrer Blehl's *The White Stone* (Petersham, MA: St. Bede's Publications, 1993), p. 73.

Chapter Five. The Prodigal Son and Other Stories About Following Jesus

1. Teresa of Avila, *De libro vitae*, cap. 22, 6–7, 14.

2. Cited in Vincent Ferrer Blehl's *The White Stone* (Petersham, MA: St. Bede's Publications, 1993), pp. 37–39.

3. Edward J. Farrell, *The Father Is Very Fond of Me* (NJ: Dimension Books, 1975), p. 5.

4. Taken from Paul A. Holmes, "Broken Glass" *America*, 9 September 1995, p. 22.

5. We will closely follow here the treatment of conversion in Ronald D. Witherup's *Conversion in the New Testament* (Collegeville, MN: The Liturgical Press, 1994), pp. 44–56.

6. Ibid., p. 55.

7. Ibid., p. 48.

8. Evelyn Waugh, *Brideshead Revisited* (Boston: Little, Brown and Co., 1982), p. 24.

Chapter Six. Jesus the Lord—and Evil

1. Joseph Cardinal Bernardin, *The Gift of Life* (Chicago: Loyola Press, 1997), pp. 151–52.

Chapter Seven. The Beloved Disciple

1. Joan Chittister, O.S.B., *The Fire in These Ashes* (Kansas City, MO: Sheed and Ward, 1995), p. 32.

2. This information that he "was known to the high priest" probably gave rise to the second-century tradition that John (thought to be the disciple) was a priest.

3. Raymond E. Brown, S.S., explains that "In the tradition (1 Cor 15:5; Lk 24:34), Simon Peter was the first among the disciples of Jesus to see the risen Jesus. John does not violate that but still exemplifies his peculiar emphasis: Throughout the latter part of the Gospel the unnamed Beloved Disciple, the one particularly loved by Jesus, is closer than Peter to the master. In John 20:3–10, where Peter and the Beloved Disciple go to the tomb, neither sees Jesus; but the Beloved Disciple comes to faith without an appearance of the risen One." *Reading the Gospels with the Church* (Cincinnati: St. Anthony Messenger Press, 1996), p. 73.

4. Raymond E. Brown, S.S., *The Gospel and Epistles of John* (Collegeville, MN: The Liturgical Press, 1988), p. 103.

5. In his *Death of the Messiah*, vol. 2 (New York: Doubleday, 1994), Raymond E. Brown points out that a more accurate rendering of this phrase is that the disciple took Mary "into his own" (see pp. 1023–25).

6. Brown, *Reading the Gospels,* pp. 74–75.

7. Nikos Kazantzakis, *St. Francis,* trans. P. A. Bien (New York: Simon and Schuster, 1962), p. 98.

ILLUMINATIONBOOKS

Other Books in the Series

Love God...Clean House...Help Others
by Duane F. Reinert, O.F.M. Cap.

Along Your Desert Journey
by Robert M. Hamma

Appreciating God's Creation Through Scripture
by Alice L. Laffey

Let Yourself Be Loved
by Phillip Bennett

Facing Discouragement
by Kathleen Fischer and Thomas Hart

Living Simply in an Anxious World
by Robert J. Wicks

A Rainy Afternoon with God
by Catherine B. Cawley

Time, A Collection of Fragile Moments
by Joan Monahan

15 Ways to Nourish Your Faith
by Susan Shannon Davies

God Lives Next Door
by Lyle K. Weiss

Advance Praise for *Following in the Footsteps of Jesus*

"The Bible offers magnificent examples of what is required to be a disciple, walking on the path that leads to God—a path that Jesus illuminated so clearly. This book draws on those examples with faithful perception and insight, and gives most helpful guidance. It is encouraging to see the Bible put to the service of spiritual growth in this way."

> *—Raymond E. Brown*
> *Auburn Distinguished Professor Emeritus*
> *of Biblical Studies*
> *Union Theological Seminary (NYC)*

"*Following in the Footsteps of Jesus* is a delightful blend of perceptive interpretation of Scripture and thoughtful reflection on the moral imperatives that flow from the Bible. Through encounters with biblical characters, Coleman and Pettingill offer readers an opportunity to test out their own discipleship and embrace the need for ongoing conversion."

> *—Ronald D. Witherup, S.S.*
> *Provincial, U.S. Province of Sulpicians*